SECRETS TO AVOIDING "THE KNOW IT ALL" eCommerce GURUS

Understanding Experts and How to Stay Away From All The Drama and Trouble

By

Anonymous Thrifter

© Copyright 2020

All rights reserved

No part of this publication that, except in the case of short quotations used in critical reviews in some other non-commercial applications, be reproduced, circulated or transmitted in any way or by any means, including by photocopying, recording or other electronic or mechanical means or by any method of storage and recovery of information without the prior written permission of the publisher.

DISCLAIMER

This document is geared towards providing exact and suitable information in regards to the topic and issue covered in this book. The publication is sold on the concept that the publisher is not required to render an accounting, officially allowed, or otherwise qualified service. If advice is necessary, legal, or professionals, a practiced individual in the profession should be called.

From a Declaration of Principles which was accepted and approved equally by a Committee of the American Bar Association and a Committee of Publishers and Associations.

In no way is it legal to reproduce, duplicate, from, or transmit any part of this document by either a printed format or electronic means. Recording of this publication is highly prohibited, and any storage of this document is not allowed unless with written permission from the publisher. All rights reserved.

The information provided herein is stated to be truthful and consistent, in that any liability, in terms of inattention or otherwise, by any usage or abuse of any policies, processes, or directions contained within is the solitary and utter responsibility of the recipient reader. Under no circumstances will any legal responsibility or blame be held against the publisher for any reparation, damages, or monetary loss due to the information herein, either directly or indirectly.

The respective author owns all copyrights not held by the publisher.

The information herein is offered for informational purposes solely and is universal as so.

The presentation of the information is without a contract or any type of guarantee assurance.

ACKNOWLEDGEMENTS

All acknowledgments go to my fellow Thrifters and Sellers, new and experienced, who need a little guidance and to those who understand what this book is all about.

FOREWORD

Firstly, I thank you for taking the step of trusting me and deciding to purchase/read this life-transforming eBook. Thanks for spending your time and resources on this material.

I can assure you exact results if you will diligently follow the precise blueprint; I lay bare in the information manual you are currently reading. It has transformed lives, and I firmly believe it will equally transform your own life too.

All the information I present in this Do It Yourself (DIY) piece is easy to digest and practice. I believe it will save a lot of headaches.

INTRODUCTION

I am an online seller with over 20 years of experience in this field. I have been inspired by many, and let down by many. I have seen the best and the worst in people in this industry over the years. Both online and in person, I have seen drama unfold and divide the camps to the point that business relationships were destroyed, friendships were shattered and most of a community put in turmoil. This is not what we should strive for in our business(es).

It is interesting to acknowledge the remarkable resourcefulness of advances in technology and the digital world how those inventions have made many business transactions easier as opposed to the ancient times where you have to input high physical energy to get your products and services across to those who would appreciate it. However, people are making use of the Internet for their business entities. The Internet has been one of the greatest blessings of all times as the world is going digital and electronic, and whoever will thrive in the world of commerce and business must be updated in the advances experienced in the world of the Internet. Ignorance of the technological world is not excusable as its effects will surely be felt in your endeavors;

ignorance is unpardonably leaving us all with the only option to get ourselves wired up to enjoy the beautiful world of the Internet.

eCommerce, as it were, is a popular term for electronic commerce or internet commerce. The name is expressly mentioned and is the gathering of internet buyers and sellers. This covers goods and services purchases, the transfer of funds, and data sharing. It assuredly remains a relatively new, emerging, and continuously changing area of information technology and business management. Amazingly, eCommerce is one of the fastest-growing industries in the global community of the economy. It grows almost 23 percent each year, according to an estimate. And by the end of this decade, it is predicted to be a $27 trillion industry; this probable prediction has drawn the attention of many world leaders, officials, and business tycoons as they give their time, energy, concentration, and investments into this emerging system of trade.

TABLE OF CONTENTS

CHAPTER 1
Who are the eCommerce experts?   11

CHAPTER 2
Importance of experts in your field and learn from them   22

CHAPTER 3
Vulnerabilities of experts   33

CHAPTER 4
How to identify experts with a bad attitude   42

CHAPTER 5
Leaning on the shoulders of experts   46

CHAPTER 6
Pros and cons of experts in e-commerce   54

CHAPTER 7
How to play safe when with gurus in a conference   64

CHAPTER 8
How to address an expert or guru   71

CHAPTER 9
How to act like an expert in a conference without being intimidated   78

CHAPTER 10
Disadvantages of having a clash with an expert in a conference   82

CHAPTER 11
Conclusion   93

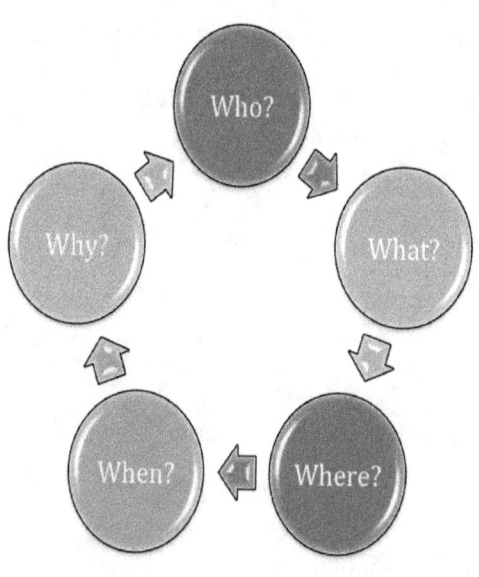

CHAPTER 1

Who are the eCommerce Experts?

In every field in the world, as there are first expositions that a beginner could easily access and comprehend, in the same vein, there is some in-depth knowledge not exposed to beginners, not because they are also not a bonafide member of the field. Still, they are usually unable to handle professional matters in the same field. These same realities find expression in the world of eCommerce as some are called EXPERTS; these have gone through professional pieces of training and have acquired many thorough skills that could deal with different challenges in the world of internet commerce; their extensive experiences have separated them from the newbies. Meeting an eCommerce expert is almost always the ambition of newbies so they could engage them in reasonable conversations and draw from their wealth of wisdom in the sphere of eCommerce.

There are so many criteria that separate an expert from a beginner in the eCommerce industry. Still, to be realistic, an expert was once a beginner, and it is not far-fetched for a beginner to also emerge as an eCommerce expert if the beginner can devote himself/herself to the secrets embedded in this book. The eCommerce leader is the chief manager of the organization's electronic storefront. Their heartfelt mandate is to drive new traffic, create and deliver an extensive online experience that will endear users to the brand, and turn visitors into repeat customers while maximizing overall profitability of the online business; because eCommerce is getting more influential in the world of business development and global trading system, therefore, the obligations of an eCommerce professional are wide-ranging, including persuasive techniques, website development, user experience, maintenance, analytics, security, operations, sound technology, and oversight of third-party service providers and commitment to customer care services. They also act as an internal ambassador to rally other activities of the company behind the business's eCommerce site. Any management position, regardless of the level, requires doggedness and astute leadership, playing a pivotal role in departmental and overall business performance.

Furthermore, an eCommerce expert works closely with website developers and oversees the selection of platforms for execution of eCommerce ideas, solutions, verification, online payment systems, authentication, security, and a display of other technologies required to operate a web-based business. However, it is initially expedient to explain who an expert is, you have always believed that expertise in eCommerce is something hard to come by; yet if you can patiently go through the skills and wisdom that make an expert, you will be amazed how easily you could also emerge as an expert; therefore, my first assignment is to explain who an expert is. But besides the technical skills, what else does it cost you to be a competent eCommerce expert? Check out the following attributes and nuggets that make an expert.

Vision Driven Mindset

The eCommerce expert holds the company's eCommerce vision, and he/she is never void of insight, foresight, and hindsight concerning the company involvement. He/she seeks long-term market potential, which affords him/her the ability to checkmate any hitch that could emerge later and firmly always stays on the lookout for business opportunities. They're experts at employing research and customer data to drive the business. They think "beyond the horizon" in any language—their vision births a level of strong experience to handle and manage the company judiciously and prudently. You want concrete examples from those candidates that demonstrate these competencies.

Strong Search Engine Optimization (SEO) Prowess

The oxygen upon which a site survives is encoded in the SEO. (I've heard the nickname SECO called "spider food".) Experts must explicitly comprehend the current requirements for top SERPs. Have you ever wondered why some sites move up in the search engines? It is the work of an experienced hand in search engine optimization. It is not just enough for the eCommerce professional to type a blog or two, or for their manager to haphazardly create a click ad campaign with the hopes of driving traffic and securing sales. A deep understanding of SEO algorithms for Google, Wikipedia, and Yahoo is required. Without such intimate knowledge, the site(s) will not be seen, and sales will plummet. This is one of the necessary skills an expert acquires.

Solution Giver

One of the best ways to be an expert is to sell solutions; an expert is never indifferent to any matter as regards their work; they are always looking out for any loopholes or problems to solve. If you were to ask the top marketing percentile how they have become successful in business, many would answer that they found the solution to the problem and presented it to the world. It is not that they are selling a product or a service; they are selling a solution. Remember that people want to see solutions and not stories. Yes, they have something for sale, but at the end of the day, a person wants to be able to look back and say, "Oh, amazing! I solved this problem!".

Strong Persuasive Skills

Usually, people are moved and compelled by persuasions. When someone decides to trade online, he or she is interested in a product that could best suit his/her demand, and they will use price comparison websites as well as reviews to find the best deals. The successful eCommerce expert will have the attribute to persuade the client that the expense is worth it with much reassurance of how satisfied he/she would feel after making demands. Whether this is through showcasing the product better than the competitor, through much online teaching and support, or through just having a superior product, the manager's job is to secure the sale and win over the customer's heart.

These aforementioned attributes are must-haves for every expert. Whenever you notice these attributes in an individual in the world of eCommerce, be certain you are in training with an expert who has bagged loads of experiences, which could be pivotal for uplifting the world of eCommerce.

CHAPTER 2

Importance of Experts in Your Field, and Learn from Them

The survival of knowledge is in its transfer to coming generation because knowledge in a field or sphere of life can be lost if not guided, maintained and transferred to the appropriate levels; many professionals in the different field have learned this reality of life which has spurred them to establish institutions, schools of learning and teaching centers for the upcoming generations so they could be participants and beneficiaries of their life-long earned experiences and expertise.

An expert can be believed, by exposure, reliable credentials, various training, educational status, professional affiliation, publication or experience, to have unique knowledge of a subject beyond that of the average person, sufficient that others may officially rely upon the individual's opinion on that topic. All these credentials have placed experts at a level where their importance cannot be overemphasized; there are many reasons why experts are essential in a particular field. Is it almost always impossible for a sphere of knowledge to be publicized, understood, and appreciated if there is no expertise involved?

Invariably, the breakthrough of a field is founded, determined, and sustained by the devotion of the experts involved in such fields.

Professionals in eCommerce have brought loads of milestones and prospects to the world of internet commerce, and their influence cannot be handled with levity based on the sacrifice they have made in making eCommerce one of the fastest-growing hubs of institutions in the global economy. Interestingly, the only reason why people would gladly create passionate interests in this industry is based on the breakthroughs that have been recorded so far in your internet eCommerce systems; meanwhile, the laurels for these breakthroughs are from those who by much expertise have hit the capstone.

Well, the primary reason for any industry even eCommerce is to satisfy the needs and demands of clients and to receive their unending approvals, acknowledgments, and endorsements in subsequent inventions, programs, and services rendered by the company, this reason alone has already shifted the attention of an eCommerce company from themselves to their clients. The importance of experts is based on clients' disposition and public acceptance.

Clients trust experts: The subject of trust is the sole entity for people's commitment to a course, and a society where trust is lost; consequently confidence, confidence, and commitment are also lost. People are more likely to believe your recommendation or suggestion when you know more. Meanwhile, experts are considered to understand in a broad sense than an average person in a field. People tend to trust them more than any other person.

They earn more patronage from clients: In some situations, this is the starting point of the first point, so that you can trust more closely in a deeper understanding of your subject and make your pick a product or service more appealing and persuasive. This is especially so if you are an expert with a strong sense of ethics without jeopardizing the standards that your field represents. More opportunities for posting guests to major sites are also available. When you recognize that you have an exceptionally knowledgeable subject, this is so much easier. Experts may gain media attention. We are dealing with eCommerce, which is completely digital and has all processes achieved online. Both crude and new media depend on experts to flesh out relatable stories. Eventually, people will figure out where the expert's social profiles are and want to connect with them. Of course, this goes much more effectively if he/she is diligent at what he/she does. People will want to share their thoughts and knowledge with the expert and develop a cordial connection with them. Either way, incoming links are still the main driver in the SEO rankings.

Pure gold is more comfortable to draw high-quality natural bonds. Also, more tweets, plus ones, and likes will spread the message further every day for experts. It is nice that they may receive invitations to be on TV or radio, or that publishers can ask the expert to share their insight into a novel. Regardless of how it takes form, it will give them the attention they deserve and respect anywhere in the world to be considered an "expert."

Experts Connect: Being known as an expert tends to attract smart, motivated employees who can make a tremendous difference in their business. Other experts are attracted to other experts. And this could be open to the audience's introduction. No specialist wants to work with a weakly investigated publisher of thin content. This would bring outflows of connection.

Their power of predictions: Both technical and fundamental analysis is at the mercy of expertise, and the inability to predict the world of eCommerce is dangerous. However, with know-how comes more knowledge of the major players in your industry, and the things they're likely to do. Even though you can't accurately predict everything, but expertise can help you get ready for change. An expert idea on the subject or topic matter will help you to understand what help you need and how to burrow your way through into limelight.

Search engines favor of quality: The changes are always significant, but they're going in a consistent direction, better quality content gets more attention. Search engines will undoubtedly improve the quality, and only high-quality content will win this political game of accuracy and impeccability. It sounds harsh to say that no one cares about you if you are not a professional, of course! This is not talking about your friends, family, or social conversations here, but winning search engines favor.

These are some of the many glaring reasons why the importance of experts cannot be overemphasized, and there is a necessity laid on newbies to learn from the hands of experts and also gain grounds or else, a beginner will continue being one; there is so much competition for expertise in the world of commerce that every beginner who wants to make groundbreaking impacts must be prepared to learn massively and voraciously yet intelligently and wisely from the eCommerce big boys.

CHAPTER 3

Vulnerabilities of The Experts

(Negative side)

Many people would think expertise in the field of eCommerce is automatically immune against all forms of weakness in the world of commerce, which sincerely is far from the truth due to many factors involved in dealing with a broad field like eCommerce. eCommerce as a technological and digital field is multidimensional. No one can claim expertise in all its forms; every expert is a specialist in eCommerce and maybe a novice in another aspect of this internet business and trade center.

The division or branches of a field is enough vulnerability for the same, even though there are benefits attached to diversification. However, the other negative side is the vulnerability of an expert in an essential category of eCommerce. We would briefly look into this diversification and check how these significant elements of their own have produced experts yet has not immune them against vulnerability which would warrant an expert to desist from overconfidence in another expert's field of exposures- this consequently is a way to encourage every expert to engage interdependence in the world of commerce than trying to be alone which sooner or later would subject them to the vulnerability of all forms.

Business to Business ECommerce (B2B)

Business to Business eCommerce affords small and medium enterprises with an excellent opportunity and chance to access new trades, improve its customer service, and reduce costs. They should be viewed more and regarded as speed breakers rather than road barriers. As a medium of information storage and dissemination, the Internet has and is emerging a clear winner. Its penetration rate has far outpaced the growth of other popular media such as newspapers, radio, and television. In this expertise, the companies are doing business with each other without a clash. The final consumer is not involved. So the online transactions only include wholesalers, manufacturers, and retailers.

Business to Consumers ECommerce (B2C)

Business to Consumers eCommerce is the most accepted and popular form of eCommerce. The individuals are directly involved in B2C eCommerce, and enterprises use the Internet to offer their products or services around the clock through global access. Instacart, Flipkart, Jabong and Amazon.com are an excellent example of this. These websites sell goods directly to consumers over the Internet. The two-way accessibility feature of the Internet enables operating companies to ascertain consumer preferences and buying trends without any primary intermediary. Customers can view the goods, pictures, and feedback on their websites. They then order, and the company directly ships the goods to them.

Consumer to Consumer eCommerce (C2C)

This category of eCommerce is absolutely the cyber version of the good old auction houses. Anyone who wants to sell anything has to post a message on the site, give details of the product and the expected price, and wait for an interested customer to turn up and buy it. The buyer gets in touch with the seller through the same site of access, and the deal is crossed once the amount is finalized. Here consumers are in direct contact with each other. No company is involved. It helps people sell their goods and assets directly to an interested party.

Customer to Business eCommerce (C2B)

This works by empowering the customer by strategically redefining business. An example of the C2B model of eCommerce is the site Priceline.com, which allows prospective airline travelers across the globe, tourists in need of hotel reservations, and so on. You visit its websites and indicate their preferred price for travel between any cities.

Whenever an airline decided to issue a ticket on the customers offered price, the consumer can then travel to the mentioned destination at his terms. This is the reverse of B2C, and it is a consumer to business. So the consumer provides a good or some service to the company. Say, for example, an IT freelancer who demos and sells his software to a company. This would be a C2B transaction.

Business to Employees ECommerce (B2E)

This category is more encapsulated with marketing a corporation's internal processes more efficiently. Customer care and support activities also hold ground. The requirement is that it is all self-service with applications on the web that the employees can use themselves. Business to Employees

ECommerce (B2E) this is concerned more with marketing a corporation's internal processes more efficiently. Customer care and support activities also hold ground. The requirement is that it is all self-service with applications on the web that the employees can use themselves.

The effect of specialty renders every expert vulnerable to other categories of eCommerce services, as it is to be conceived that no man can stand as an expert in all aspects of eCommerce. The vulnerability of eCommerce is founded upon its diversification in different aspects of the digital economy around the world.

CHAPTER 4

How To Identify Experts With A Bad Attitude

Poisonous blends are low morality, tragedy, and disaster, distrust, and terror. You probably wonder how anyone can survive on them all! These people, however, exist globally and are seldom avoidable, especially in eCommerce.

This doesn't mean you won't have moments of anonymity and trust. But don't permit thoughts as a practical person because they take over your life. You let positive thinking shine out any negative to stop spiraling out of control in situations.

Even though they are experts in this field, especially in eCommerce, they can exhibit some characteristics among all the participants of a conference or seminar that show their attitude and this type of people (experts) that you should pay attention to.

They complain a great deal: People with bad attitudes prefer to feel that someone needs to look at problems and do themselves. In general, you are a victim of unfair issues for others, and they will make you feel, especially beginners scorned by important and abundant factors, like energy loss, imagination, or hard work.

Enjoy secrecy: If you meet an expert at a conference, there can be a long discussion. They think so much about being posted about themselves and fear that it is used somehow against them. They never think it would be good to use what they say.

They instead will keep vital information to themselves and act like they know nothing about it.

You have to have a thick skin: Those with bad behaviors are usually too open to criticism and even lousy. Innocent comments are viewed as negative or disgusting. For instance, a cynical can find offensive jokes, especially if it relates to them in away.

The only opinion he holds is his: a clear indicator that he's wrong is that the statement he makes is passed through a psychological filter asking: "What does this mean about me?

Training

Knowledge
useful abiliti~~es~~.
backbone of co
quired for a tr

CHAPTER 5

Leaning on The Shoulders of Experts

There is a common saying that no one is an island of knowledge; therefore, everyone strives to learn one or two things from those that have gone ahead of them. The world of eCommerce is a bit complex but could be made simplified through the hands of experts who have gone ahead. Due to the level of expertise, they have acquired, the credentials they have and their ability to proffer solution to diverse, complicated problems in the world of eCommerce; they are worthy of emulation for newbies to tread the pathway that brought them to where they are and even skyrockets into greater stardom than them.

Need to rest on the shoulders of experts or professionals cannot be denied either can it be overstated at any point in the journey. Most of the time, you are given the leverage to begin where they stopped. That is, their peak of success would likely be your foundation of breakthrough, making mentoring a necessity and not an option.

To establish that point further, you would notice that what confers the prowess and skill used by an expert to tackle a problem is based on a knowledge he possesses that is usually not exposed to the public attention making them invariably a step higher than you are. It is only through mentoring that you could be trusted to partake in their secret codes of proffering solutions and rendering indispensable assistance to their clients.

When it comes to attracting an expert that would be of essential help to you, there are a few things you can do to stand out and get the attention of someone that matters. In all my years of building an enviable eCommerce carrier, I can tell you the mentors on my path contributed largely to my successes. Well, it might be disgusting to stay under a harsh mentor, but the profits gained at the end of the day outweigh the processes you pass through, thereby the glory is worth the investments of learning.

An expert can be any person with experience, skills, and expertise in an area of knowledge that could help your career. Usually, the process of teaching involves information you can't learn in books or come across online, so it's vitally important that you pick his or her brain to get that "Intel." However, to find that mentor, you have to be inquisitive; You have to put yourself out there, show your interest to learn, and built a rapport that makes a sound and cordial relationship that could last for a lifetime.

Search for experts in your field of interest in eCommerce

Finding the right professional is all about understanding what it is you want to learn. You already know what you want to do with digital commerce; therefore, look at the marketplace and target some players in your business area that you aspire to be like, especially those you know their track records, tested, and trusted. Is there someone in your network who's doing what you want to be doing one day excellently? If so, reach out to them. You don't have to walk up and say, "Will you be my mentor?"-just establish a relationship and ask for advice. Be interested in asking questions, and I mean reasonable questions that could heartily catch the attention of that expert to your side to the end that he also sees someone he could intelligently breed and bring up.

Most people misunderstand and misinterpret the concept of teaching. It usually starts with a single question and then grows organically from there. It's not about someone pulling you aside and saying, "I want to mentor you." It's about you asking the right questions at the right time, and proving that you're willing to learn and improve.

Be willing to be wrong

It is essential not to allow your leader to lose interest in you due to your inability to yield to corrections; you must know that you are just coming up and would need some improvements over time; you should reassess the likelihood of you meeting your goals. The fact that you're mistaken doesn't mean you have failed, and it only means you need to learn something important.

Be humble

Humility is never demoralizing yourself but a state of mind to learn from an old-timer or mentor even if you have an edge in any area than him so far you are a novice in the realm of the sphere you are willing to learn. Believe in yourself, but talk to people further along than you. The bottom of the matter here is not about discouraging you from reaching the capstone, but even the noblest and fruitful people have mentors and people they turn to for advice and insight. When you make it big, find a mentor for dealing with success.

CHAPTER 6

Pros and Cons of Experts in Ecommerce

For every positive influence, eCommerce experts could be wisely harnessed for your profiting. Experts according to the last CHAPTERs are shoulders to lean on; they are trained through which we could be carried to the place where we desired in the eCommerce world, the following points are pros of experts in eCommerce:

Pros of experts in eCommerce

Effective service

The truth is that eCommerce experts have the beautiful advantage of being able to best serve the company in roles that give it regular opportunities to draw on their specialist knowledge. This helps them to "keep themselves in the form" and maintain the abilities that differentiate them from other team members. In places where the various ideas can be extended under consideration — typical governance and technical roles — we found expert users are most helpful. As members of the board and inventors, the wealth of experience of experts is disabled so as not to provide ideas and perspectives.

They are least successful in roles where they are unable to demonstrate their expertise; so when considering where experts belong in your company, ask yourself, "Is this a role that focuses more on generating a variety of ideas or one that focuses on selecting from among ideas?" which usually is useful when the latter is implemented.

Quality work

Experts can produce good content for your site of trade transactions because you need some compelling images and different ads to keep your eCommerce business profiles engaging and captivating. This grants you the privilege of receiving training on the quality based level, empowering you to be able to contend with the same sets of professionals in the same field. ECommerce experts know how to encourage audience participation and engagement in different ways beyond generic postings, which consequently rubs off on you to be able to do the same.

Tracking & Measure

Experts could teach and help set up desirable pixels, conversion tracking codes, marketing audiences, and more. This will enable you to determine how an audience is progressing through the marketing funnel from product view, lead; add to cart, and sale.

The cons of experts in eCommerce

An unskillful person in the world of digital commerce might suggest that the more experts, the better. The just uttered statement is not always accurate; having more captains on a ship is a pathway to bury the ship in the body of waters. More so, the fact that experts are indispensable does not mean they are without their flaws.

Psychological entrenchment

As experts gain more in-depth expertise in an area, they tend to acquire more accurate, concise, and detailed knowledge but also become less flexible in their thinking and less likely to change their perspective even if they are not correct. Therefore, expert boards may be less effective in responding to new or unexpected circumstances. Indeed, research indicates that management teams consisting of many veterans in business are less agile in adapting to competitive shifts, which is not ideal for learning newbies.

Overconfidence

Overconfidence is a negative attitude that vaguely affects eCommerce experts; they usually think they could never be taken aback by some situations that are often simple but tricky to deal with, especially in satisfying the needs of clients. It is a common problem in expert judgment that affects experts in a wide range of fields. One member of the board, for instance, explained in banking. This makes boards of many non-expert executives more suspicious. "They need more reporting and review." And they always reply, "We won't make a decision today, because you haven't provided us with adequate details for decision-making." Overconfidence is the "I do KNOW" syndrome that renders experts vulnerable to simple mistakes, which may cause a massive wreck on the eCommerce system.

Task conflict

In a situation where different facts, holistic views, diverse viewpoints, ideas, and opinions about the decisions faced are needed to determine the way out selectively. Some amount of task conflict is essential because it allows the board to explore and discuss more alternatives. But research suggests that a high proportion of domain experts can suppress task conflict because non-expert directors may defer too much to experts' judgment. And most of the time, it is difficult to challenge experts to justify the available assumptions and consider alternatives. Usually, when you see something you don't like, you are afraid to bring it up because an expert is fully involved and questioning his view could to him mean being rude.

Inability to manage your relationship with experts

Though experts are incredibly accurate and good at what they do, they often wander down paths that you may not want to go; they might want to force you to move in a glaringly negative path they tread. An expert can be intimidating. You might feel that you've come across the expertise needed for your growth; you need to let them do what they recommend, yet they would still be determined to make you follow suit. The expert works with you, trains you, and you almost always find it hard to ensure they work in your best interest and not the best interest of the so-called expert.

CHAPTER 7

How to Play Safe When with Gurus in A Conference

In any workplace, gurus or experts are identified. In whatever type you can think of, troublesome people come. But how difficult it is to deal with others depends very much on factors such as self-esteem, every day working closely with them, and professional bravery.

It is easier to work with people who are problematic if the person is typically negative or if the conduct affects more than one person.

It is much easier to negotiate with challenging individuals who deliberately question their professional integrity, take credit for their efforts, or threaten them personally.

Every conference, field, or career is made up of challenging people, experts, or gurus. It's a skill worth developing to negotiate with challenging men, bosses, experts, and Experts. It is frustrating but worthwhile to deal with tough conferences.

Through enhancing your ability to communicate with people at work, you can greatly boost your working environment and morality. It also strengthens the workspace for all other people when facing the challenges created by troublesome Gurus.

Thankfully, when you attend a seminar or conference, you spend time with virtual people you don't know in person, so many experts and gurus in your field. However, you need additional skills in the repertoire of interpersonal abilities if you come in clash with an expert or Guru.

The problem is that people have pride and fear and are encircled by cleverer people than you can make them feel bad. Naturally, few can readily admit it. However, even this simple advice is ignored by people. Only the best of us, when surrounded by geniuses, can see their faith diminishing.

Know Your Strengths

It's normal for all these people to be larger and more experienced as a novice or novice in an eCommerce field and to see many experts or Guru at the seminar if you're fortunate enough! And he would most probably think it wrong to continue to hold his line to prevent problems. Concentrate on your knowledge and expertise system and confidence in yourself. You will, therefore, prevent bullying.

Take Your Stand

You will be first forced to cover your ignorance, as you are surrounded by smart men, but this is the wrong way. You're never going to know if you don't ask questions.

"It's far easier to appear uninformed than to make you sound like you know something you don't know, which will once again torment you."

Take Your Time

Feeling relaxed in a group of gurus does not take place overnight at a seminar or conference. It can be a long road to get to know and learn from genuinely intelligent employees. Don't plan to wake up and feel fine all about one week later.

'It has taken him several years to be one of the biggest men, don't run into a meeting or talking to someone at a lecture or conference, take the time to focus. Not all experts will pleasantly take your approach.

Don't Compete

The more competitive you become, the less you learn and do. "Don't start fighting. It will be much easier to know the day you agree that there will always be smarter men."

Take care of your collection's diversity. You won't necessarily beat the experts, but from the left-field, you might take this primary insight. Seek to take all the details you can from outside so that from time to time, you can take a different perspective without being utterly idiotic.

CHAPTER 8

How to Address an Expert or Guru

Anyone who wants to excel in eCommerce should find a profession or Guru to guide them. Obtaining your opinion and advice from someone who knows what you want would, in many ways, benefit you. You avoid heartburn and expensive naive errors.

But how do you begin to talk? Social networking, hangouts, and conferences have made contact with the professionals or Guru, who encourage us simpler than ever. While some experts can be nicer to approach, some can be very mean and rude; however, you need to be very careful with your approach.

Before you ask a question, try answering it yourself

Studying a subject makes more sense before you believe like you well know it, and then turn to an Expert or Guru. The viewpoint you are looking for is tightened up. To be honest, most experts are not prepared to answer more than one question. So do it right. So get it right!

Briefly explain who you are

The contents of your conversation are always helpful. Who are you? Why are you trying to sit or have a conversation with me for a moment? Experts would like to know. There is no need for a long breathless clarification or introduction. Just something very precise like something as easy as your name, and aspiring eCommerce professional or something very brief about you." You'll be humanized if you do that. Most importantly, you need to be precise in explaining your identity.

A little flattery will get you far.

What expert listens most to is that what they do is valued? It's a simple trick to get their attention by telling them that you love their last work or that you bought their course or joined their membership program. They feel impressed by themselves and want to hear more. Try to be as accurate as possible; otherwise, you will get them bored.

Ask questions that are clearly defined, but not necessarily specific to your intentions

Experts cannot weigh the exact scenario you are in, as this would not be sincere. They just don't know enough about you or what situation you are in, and they wouldn't want to give bad advice to anyone. Instead, focus on asking more general questions, where they can capture your thoughts from easily, else you stand a chance at annoying them with your question.

Be even-keeled

I can't stress that enough! You know what you want, isn't it? Concentrate on beginning a conversation rather than verifying an opinion.

When people disclose something they already think as they first ask about even a subject, I'm careful when talk begins. The truth is it's not going to be a major talk.

Experts would just like to say things and don't convince you. There is no reason you will ask a question when you already have your own conformed opinions.

Double-check how to spell their names

Addressing an expert via messages or notes in a conference isn't bad. Still, with the nature of some, they can tear up your note and bin it once their name is seen to be wrongly written without even reading up the rest of your message, pronouncing and writing the names of this expert is very important if you want to have a conversation with them, without pulling any issues to yourself.

"BE HUMBLE IN YOUR CONFIDENCE YET COURAGEOUS IN YOUR CHARACTER."

CHAPTER 9

How to Act Like an Expert in A Conference Without Being Intimidated by Anyone

Experts are listed as Experts in all fields. They are highly qualified, widely known, and able to understand and support others in all aspects of their work. They are people we turn or look up to for guidance, new ideas on business development, and help us to resolve the obvious while solving problems.

Experts are not on everybody's path; they are ready to make improvements to better the industry. To be an expert, abandon harm and explore new methods. After finding a better alternative, teach them to be better and more effective.

If your colleagues do not identify you as such, you cannot become an expert. That is why it is essential to have a relationship. When approachable, personalized, and respectful, experts are most active. Do not create a community, but rather build a community that can draw on your experience and fosters universal success. He is catapulted to the top by his relationships and by admiration.

To avoid having any issues with Gurus in a conference or seminar, you need to act like one; appearing inferior can spur rooms for insult, attitudes, or rudeness from other people or so-called gurus in the conference. To stay safe and move more freely, you need to act like one, and this is nothing something you activate, you need to be consistent. You are not competing, but you want to save your name from insult or embarrassment.

- Speak up
- Think before you speak
- Never feel inferior
- Stand up when you speak
- A statement is not a question; don't express yourself asking a question when you just made a statement.
- Study grammar
- Don't overdo it
- Don't just answer their questions -- Take charge instead
- Asking questions that convey expertise
- Most importantly, show confidence.

CHAPTER 10

Disadvantages of Having A Clash with An Expert in A Conference

As useful as the help an expert is in building your business, it can be your doom as well. There are many Guru out there with an appalling attitude, and they can make or mar your career with significant influence. If you are in a conference with any, it is best to be very careful without your approach, then being careless.

Expert are always there to help, but not all are there in the real sense at a point in time, if you stumble upon an expert in a conference and you both have a clash, here is what is at stake for you.

1. Affect your Reputation

2. Makes you Less Creative

3. Low Self-esteem

Affects Your Reputation

Your credibility is your business's most crucial element. It influences anything from the number of social media backers to overall sales. There are just a few more advantages of a strong reputation:

- More opportunities for business.
- Lower exchange interest.
- Lower expense of advertisement.

People want to make the right decision and choose the individual or organization that seems to have a better reputation. If you apply for a job or win business opportunities, your business results are affected by a good reputation.

Incidents occur that can significantly harm your business if you have a clash with some experts at the conference. However, it is the importance of reputational damage that can cost you more than you can imagine.

If your business is just coming to limelight, and you have a clash with an expert, it can affect your growth as you will have no one to do business with you or relate with you.

But what are the real effects of reputational damage? First; Customer reliability in you based on whatever reaction the expert you had a clash with must have done or bothered by an interruption that has not been dealt with appropriately; they are likely to take their business to another person.

Customers and peers can also share their anger on social media platforms, which further damages you and your business reputation.

Secondly, businesses may be required to compensate those you are presently dealing with who will most likely withdraw from engaging in any transaction with you, which could lead to debt.

Makes You Less Creative

After a damaged reputation, the situation can push you into many other problems, such as being less creative. However, the consequences of less creativity;

It's a little dull, but we have to say it. The original vision is groundbreaking. Nothing can be innovated without this imaginative dream. It's like trying to make an egg-free omelet. It will not work. It does not work.

A lack of specific written priorities and a comprehensive written action plan are the main hindrance to innovative thinking. There is a legitimate fear of failure or loss, the fear of mistake, mistake, or the loss of money or time. It is the possibility of failure that paralyzes practice, anticipates failure, and is the principal reason why the problem is not solved.

The fear of criticism or mockery, disrespect, or refusal is the fear of being dumb or stupid.

This is caused by the urge of people who you don't know or who don't care to be accepted, remembered by others.

The implicit compulsion to keep up with what you have done or said before is the fear of just doing something new or unusual. This homeostatic drive stops people from getting all they can and can do. You will lose your strength or energy like a muscle that does not exercise if you don't continually stimulate your mind with new thoughts and knowledge. Your idea is passive and reactive rather than proactively and creatively thinking.

Low Self-Esteem

Knowledge of the effects of low Self-esteem starts with self-esteem itself. Why does it matter so much? What is its shortcoming so dangerous?

Put merely, self-esteem is a way of thinking. This is self-esteem and happiness. It's self-esteem, necessarily.

You feel relaxed, driven, and inspired when you have self-esteem and good self-esteem. Because if you don't, your self-confidence will be weakened, and there will be a list of consequences. You can feel like your life has been shot.

Self-esteem has a clear link with mood. You can feel a variety of negative sentiments when it decreases sorrow, guilt, fear, frustration, loneliness, stress, even depression. Everybody has cycles of negative emotion, but it is especially difficult for a person with low self-esteem to shake off him and often combined.

Hating yourself: It would be difficult to forgive yourself if perhaps you hate yourself, or maybe because of your thoughts or deeds. When you hate your body, it's because you feel incapable of caring for yourself and permitting yourself not to look after yourself that you end up wondering how to do in relationships and work.

To assume that you have nothing to offer: It represents a deep sense of worthlessness. It is also "heroic" and even unachievable for you to see the attributes and talents of others as superior to your own. You might think that nobody cares what you believe, feel, or give if you have problems with the effects of low self-esteem. Also, it can lead to isolation, uncertainty, dedication and engagement, and finally, pent-up frustration. Everyone has something to offer.

All this can be saturated with just on the act of having a clash with an expert in a conference or seminar and is enough to ruin your life or your business. This does not disprove the advantage of learning from an expert or Guru in eCommerce, as it has a positive influence.

You are unable to change anything to believe it: This lie leads naturally to anxiety and restlessness, and it becomes your dwarf agony and rage when it is compounded by your conviction that your feelings do not matter to others.

CHAPTER 11

Conclusion

You must understand that, as an expert, it is essential to growing our business(es). As we need their guides and blueprints to succeed, especially in eCommerce, it can be awful if the negative side is turned towards us.

Being an expert does not make your attitude or your reaction to people any kinder or less helpful, there are many experts with a lousy approach who will take up every little situation they see as an insult, such as;

- Asking them too many questions;
- Pointing out their errors;
- Going against their point of view in a conference discussion;

- Telling them areas where you think they can develop better.

Regardless of how you express yourself, they will feel insulted and will take it up very badly. However, with due diligence, you need to approach any expert carefully, asking them only necessary questions, and now a conversation that spurs anger or bitterness within them.

You should observe an expert before approaching them to be on a safer side, **not all experts are worth your stand or time**. Take time to listen to others who have dealt with the same actions, fears and experience.

Understanding your self-esteem will give you a bonus hand in making yourself appear as an expert also.

Shhhhh!

www.ingramcontent.com/pod-product-compliance
Lightning Source LLC
Chambersburg PA
CBHW070251220526
45465CB00004B/1577